Friends for Life

EDITED BY SARAH ARAK

Introduction

OF ALL THE RELATIONSHIPS WE EXPERIENCE IN LIFE, NONE are more important than our friendships. We value our friends so deeply because they allow us the freedom to be ourselves without fear of judgment or criticism. Friendship takes time to establish, but once in place, it is one of the most comfortable and enjoyable relationships we can have with another person.

Unlike our family members, friends start out as complete strangers. We must therefore work at building up these interpersonal connections by talking, listening, and providing unconditional love and support. Since the act of friendship may require self-disclosure, the process often has risks. But the result is an unshakable bond of equality and loyalty that often lasts a lifetime.

From humble beginnings, fledgling acquaintances blossom into rich relationships that enhance our lives and help shape our personalities. For this reason, we owe it to our friends to let them know how terrific they are and how glad we are to have them in our lives.

IN MY FRIEND, I FIND A SECOND SELF.

—Isabel Norton

WE NEED OLD FRIENDS TO HELP US GROW OLD,

AND NEW FRIENDS TO HELP US STAY YOUNG.

—Letty Cottin Pogrebin

I CANNOT EVEN IMAGINE WHERE I WOULD BE TODAY

WERE IT NOT FOR THAT HANDFUL OF FRIENDS

WHO HAVE GIVEN ME A HEART FULL OF JOY.

LET'S FACE IT, FRIENDS MAKE LIFE A LOT MORE FUN!

—Charles R. Swindoll

A FRIEND IS SOMEONE WHO UNDERSTANDS

YOUR PAST, BELIEVES IN YOUR FUTURE,

AND ACCEPTS YOU JUST THE WAY YOU ARE.

—Author Unknown

PERHAPS THE MOST DELIGHTFUL FRIENDSHIPS

ARE THOSE IN WHICH THERE IS MUCH AGREEMENT,

MUCH DISPUTATION, AND YET MORE PERSONAL LIKING.

—George Elliot

ANYBODY CAN SAY CHARMING THINGS AND TRY TO

PLEASE AND TO FLATTER, BUT A TRUE FRIEND ALWAYS

SAYS UNPLEASANT THINGS, AND DOES NOT MIND GIVING PAIN.

INDEED, IF HE IS A REALLY TRUE FRIEND HE PREFERS IT,

FOR HE KNOWS THAT THEN HE IS DOING GOOD.

—Oscar Wilde

WE ALL NEED FRIENDS WITH WHOM WE CAN SPEAK

OF OUR DEEPEST CONCERNS, AND WHO DO NOT

FEAR TO SPEAK THE TRUTH IN LOVE TO US.

—Margaret Guenther

FRIENDSHIP IS A SINGLE SOUL

DWELLING IN TWO BODIES.

—Aristotle

FRIENDSHIP IS LIKE VITAMINS:

WE SUPPLEMENT EACH OTHER'S

MINIMUM DAILY REQUIREMENTS.

—Author Unknown

THERE IS NO SECURITY QUITE AS COMFORTABLE

AND UNDEMANDING AS THE KIND YOU

FEEL AMONG OLD FRIENDS.

— Peter Bodo

I ALWAYS FELT THAT THE GREAT HIGH, PRIVILEGE,

RELIEF AND COMFORT OF FRIENDSHIP WAS

THAT ONE HAD TO EXPLAIN NOTHING.

—Kathryn Mansfield

I GET BY WITH A LITTLE HELP

FROM MY FRIENDS.

—John Lennon

THE MOST BEAUTIFUL DISCOVERY TRUE FRIENDS

MAKE IS THAT THEY CAN GROW SEPARATELY

WITHOUT GROWING APART.

— Elisabeth Foley

A FRIEND IS THE ONE WHO COMES IN WHEN

THE WHOLE WORLD HAS GONE OUT.

— Grace Pulpit

THERE IS ONE FRIEND IN THE LIFE OF EACH OF US WHO

SEEMS NOT A SEPARATE PERSON, HOWEVER DEAR AND

BELOVED, BUT AN EXPANSION, AN INTERPRETATION,

OF ONE'S SELF, THE VERY MEANING OF ONE'S SOUL.

—Edith Wharton

IF ALL MY FRIENDS WERE TO JUMP OFF A BRIDGE,

I WOULDN'T FOLLOW. I'D BE AT THE BOTTOM

TO CATCH THEM WHEN THEY FELL.

—Author Unknown

SOME PEOPLE GO TO PRIESTS;

OTHERS TO POETRY;

I TO MY FRIENDS.

—Virginia Woolf

CONSTANT USE WILL NOT WEAR RAGGED

THE FABRIC OF FRIENDSHIP.

—Dorothy Parker

I T'S THE FRIENDS THAT YOU CAN

CALL AT 4 A.M. THAT MATTER.

— Marlene Dietrich

I COUNT MYSELF IN NOTHING ELSE SO HAPPY,

AS IN A SOUL REMEMB'RING MY GOOD

FRIENDS.

—William Shakespeare

MY BEST FRIEND IS THE ONE WHO

BRINGS OUT THE BEST IN ME.

—Henry Ford

NATURE HAS NO LOVE FOR SOLITUDE, AND

ALWAYS LEANS, AS IT WERE, ON SOME SUPPORT;

AND THE SWEETEST SUPPORT IS FOUND IN

THE MOST INTIMATE FRIENDSHIP.

— Cicero

A FRIEND IS A GIFT YOU GIVE YOURSELF.

—Robert Louis Stevenson

A FRIEND IS SOMEONE WHO SEES THROUGH YOU

AND STILL ENJOYS THE VIEW.

—Wilma Askinas

It's friendship, friendship,

Just a perfect blendship,

When other friendships have been forgot

Ours will still be hot!

— Cole Porter, *Friendship*

THE ONLY WAY TO HAVE A FRIEND

IS TO BE ONE.

—Ralph Waldo Emerson

Don't walk in front of me, I may not follow.

Don't walk behind me, I may not lead.

Walk beside me and be my friend.

— Maimonidies

ONLY FRIENDS WILL TELL YOU THE TRUTHS

YOU NEED TO HEAR TO MAKE YOUR

LIFE BEARABLE.

— Francine Du Plessix Gray

Understand that friends come and go,

but with a precious few you should hold on.

The older you get, the more you need the

people who knew you when you were young.

— Mary Schmich

HOWEVER RARE TRUE LOVE MAY BE,

IT IS LESS SO THAN TRUE FRIENDSHIP.

—La Rochefoucauld

WHO FINDS A FAITHFUL FRIEND,

FINDS A TREASURE.

—Jewish Proverb

A TRUE FRIEND IS SOMEONE WHO IS THERE

FOR YOU—WHEN THEY'D RATHER

BE ANYWHERE ELSE.

—Len Wein

FRIENDSHIP IS BORN AT THAT MOMENT

WHEN ONE PERSON SAYS TO ANOTHER,

'WHAT! YOU TOO? I THOUGHT I WAS THE ONLY ONE!'

— C.S. Lewis

TRUE FRIENDS ARE THOSE WHO LIFT YOU UP WHEN

YOUR HEART'S WINGS FORGET HOW TO FLY.

— Author Unknown

It is not so much our friends' knowledge

that helps and comforts us,

but rather the knowledge that

they will help us.

— Epicurus

Each friend represents a world in us,

a world possibly not born until they arrive,

and it is only by this meeting that

a new world is born.

—Anais Nin

ONE MEASURE OF FRIENDSHIP CONSISTS NOT IN

THE NUMBER OF THINGS FRIENDS CAN DISCUSS,

BUT IN THE NUMBER OF THINGS THEY

NEED NO LONGER MENTION.

—Clifton Fadiman

THE FINEST KIND OF FRIENDSHIP IS BETWEEN

PEOPLE WHO EXPECT A GREAT DEAL OF

EACH OTHER BUT NEVER ASK IT.

—Sylvia Bremer

HOLD A TRUE FRIEND WITH

BOTH YOUR HANDS.

— Nigerian Proverb

A FRIEND IS SOMEONE WHO KNOWS THE SONG IN

YOUR HEART, AND CAN SING IT BACK TO YOU WHEN

YOU HAVE FORGOTTEN THE WORDS.

—Author Unknown

FRIENDS ARE THE MOST

IMPORTANT INGREDIENT IN

THIS RECIPE OF LIFE.

—Author Unknown

A GOOD FRIEND IS HARD TO FIND,

HARD TO LOSE, AND

IMPOSSIBLE TO FORGET!

—Author Unknown

PHOTO CREDITS